ETHICAL
DEBATES

Privacy and Surveillance

CATH SENKER

WAYLAND

First published in 2011 by Wayland
Copyright © 2011 Wayland

Wayland
338 Euston Road
London NW1 3BH

Wayland Australia
Level 17/207 Kent Street
Sydney NSW 2000

Editor: Julia Adams
Designer: Rita Storey
Picture researcher: Diana Morris
Indexer: Rebecca Clunes

British Library Cataloguing in Publication data
Senker, Cath.
   Privacy and surveillance. -- (Ethical debates)
   1. Privacy, Right of--Juvenile literature. 2.
Electronic
   surveillance--Moral and ethical aspects--
Juvenile
   literature.
   I. Title II. Series
   323.4'48-dc22
   ISBN 978 0 7502 6568 3

Printed in China

Wayland is a division of
Hachette Children's Books,
an Hachette UK company.
www.hachette.co.uk

Picture acknowledgements:
The author and publisher would like to thank
the following agencies for allowing these
pictures to be reproduced:
Ardelean Andreea/Shutterstock: 42.
auremar/Shutterstock: 23. Glenn Copus/Evening
Standard/Rex Features: 18. Tony French/Alamy:
13. Get4Net/istockphoto: 10. Many
Godbehear/Shutterstock: 22. Adam
Hunger/Reuters: 17. Pete Jenkins/Alamy: 39.
Heino Kalis/Reuters/Corbis: 38. Keystone
USA/Zuma/Rex Features: 7. Dan Kitwood/Getty
Images: 5. Beau Lark/Corbis: 26. Keith
Leighton/Alamy: 15. Greg Mathieson/Rex
Features: 1, 36. John McDougall/AFP/Getty
Images: 40. Jeff J Mitchell/Getty Images: 16.
Dariush M./Shutterstock: 73. John
Mitchell/Alamy: 30. Monkey Business
Images/istockphoto: 27. On the Road/Alamy:
35. Pangfolio.com/Shutterstock: 28. Sabino
Parente/Shutterstock: 14. Mario Ponta/Alamy:
8. Rex Features: 25, 31, 41. Oli Scharff/Getty
Images: 33. Dmitriy Shironosov/istockphoto: 12.
67photo/Alamy: 43. Andy Stenning/Mirrorpix: 6.
Larry St Pierre/Shutterstock: 21. Kumar
Sriskandan/Alamy: 44. Jack Sullivan/Alamy: 19.
dra_swartz/istockphoto: 11.
Umbrella/Rosenblum/Virgin Films/Kobal
Collection: 45. Alvis Upitis/Getty Images: front
cover, 24. Volant/Shutterstock: 20. Bob
Watkins/Photofusion: 34. Libby Welch/Alamy: 9.
Konstantin Yuganov/istockphoto: 32.

About the Consultant: Terry Fiehn worked as a
teacher, advisory teacher and teacher trainer for
over 20 years. He is co-author of the *This is
Citizenship* series of textbooks and has written
several history textbooks and a wide range of
educational resources.He worked on the QCDA
Citizenship assessment working party and
monitoring programme.

The author would like to thank the following
for the use of their materials:
p2 case study: BBC News; p15 case study:
Aboutidentitytheft.co.uk; p23 Claire Walker

Note: The website addresses (URLs) included in this book
were valid at the time of going to press. However, because of
the nature of the Internet, it is possible that some addresses
may have changed, or sites may have changed or closed
down since publication. While the author and publishers
regret any inconvenience this may cause to the readers, no
responsibility for any such changes can be accepted by either
the author or the publishers.

contents

Real-life case study

This real-life case study highlights some of the issues that surround the debate on privacy and surveillance.

case study

WikiLeaks

Founded by Julian Assange in 2006, WikiLeaks was founded to publish secret and sensitive documents from governments and other high-profile organizations. Journalists and whistle blowers – people who raise concerns about wrongdoing in their own organization – can upload the materials anonymously. Reviewers check that the information is genuine before making it available on the WikiLeaks website.

For example, in 2010, the site released nearly 90,000 secret records from the US military operation in Afghanistan and almost 400,000 documents about Iraqi operations. They revealed the killing of civilians and torture of prisoners. In the same year, WikiLeaks published a quarter of a million leaked US embassy cables that showed how the US carried out covert surveillance of the leaders of the United Nations and had turned a blind eye to human rights abuses in countries it supported.

WikiLeaks has proved controversial. Assange and his supporters believe in freedom of information. They insist that citizens have the right to know what their government is doing. For instance, many documents illustrate the contradictions between what governments state in public and how they act behind closed doors. However, governments say that exposing their dealings endangers the privacy of the individuals involved and risks serious damage to international relations. For example, as the US ambassador to Pakistan explained, diplomats need to be able to engage in honest discussions with their colleague in the knowledge that they will remain private. Diplomats also meet with many people in the community, such as religious leaders and human rights activists. If an anti-corruption activist shared information about official misconduct in confidence and was exposed, not only would the individual's privacy be invaded, but also his or her life could be endangered.

This example illustrates some of the central issues of this book. Should people always have a right to private communications or are there cases where the invasion of privacy is in the public interest? WikiLeaks exposed the surveillance of large numbers of people. What level of surveillance can be justified to protect society from crime and wrongdoing?

It's a fact

Here are some of the WikiLeaks revelations from US embassy cables:

Iran: A number of Arab leaders called on the USA to attack Iran to stop it from developing nuclear weapons.

Sudan: President Omar al-Bashir embezzled up to US$9 billion of his country's funds.

USA: Secretary of State Hillary Clinton asked diplomats to collect DNA samples and credit card details of senior UN officials.

Was it right to expose this information or should it have remained private?

▼ WikiLeaks founder Julian Assange holds a press conference in October 2010 to tell journalists about the latest series of war logs – leaks about US military operations in Iraq.

CHAPTER 1

What are privacy and surveillance?

Before examining the ethical debate about privacy and surveillance, it is useful to define the terms and to understand how private information can be used for surveillance.

Privacy

There are many different forms of privacy. In general, it means not being watched or disturbed by other people. Private information includes personal details, such as your school records. It also includes your medical records. Communications privacy involves post, electronic communications and phone calls you receive. Territorial privacy is privacy in your own home. Article 8 of the European Convention of Human Rights (1998) states that everyone should have the right to respect for their private and family life, home and correspondence.

Surveillance

The Oxford English Dictionary defines surveillance as 'close observation, especially of a suspected person'. Methods of observation include watching, listening, filming, recording, tracking, listing people and entering their details onto databases. The different types of surveillance carried out include mass surveillance of large groups of people as well as targeted observation of specific individuals. Surveillance may be carried out openly, for example, using Closed-Circuit Television (CCTV) cameras in public places, or covertly, using undercover agents.

▼ An armed police officer carries out surveillance at Manchester Airport, UK.

▲ At an Internet café in Shenzhen City, China, volunteer supervisors monitor Internet usage. The Chinese government censors many websites, especially those that criticize the regime. This is a restriction of freedom.

Changes in surveillance

Governments have always carried out surveillance of their enemies, but also of citizens, to make sure they stay within the law. For example, Queen Elizabeth I (1558–1603) employed Sir Francis Walsingham, who was known for his spying activities. He uncovered several plots against the monarch. The Okhrana, the Russian secret police (1881–1917), planted spies in trade unions and political parties to monitor opponents to the government. From the early twentieth century, the development of magnetic recording on tape made it possible to eavesdrop on conversations.

Since the 1980s, the development of computers, the Internet and electronic devices has revolutionized how we exchange information and greatly expanded surveillance technologies. Also, since the terrorist attacks on the US of 2001 (known as the 9/11 attacks), Western governments have perceived a heightened need for surveillance to protect civilians.

viewpoints

'We are at war, and al Qaeda is not a conventional enemy. . . . Al Qaeda's plans include infiltrating [secretly entering] our cities and communities and plotting with affiliates [people linked to them] abroad to kill innocent Americans. The United States must use every tool available, consistent with the Constitution, to prevent and deter another al Qaeda attack, and the President has indicated his intent to do just that.'

The US Justice Department justifies the Terrorist Surveillance Program, which allows the National Security Agency to monitor communications in which one party is outside the US (2006)

'. . . any measures taken to counter terrorism must be proportionate and not undermine our democratic values. In particular, laws designed to protect people from the threat of terrorism, and the enforcement of these laws must be compatible with [fit with] people's rights and freedoms.'

Website of Liberty, an organization that promotes civil liberties, 2010

How private information is used for surveillance

Nowadays, government agencies record thousands of pieces of information about us every week. Most of it is simply kept on databases. This is not surveillance. However, authorities, such as the police and local government, may ask businesses or other organizations to hand over information about particular people. When other people or establishments actively observe private information that has been stored about you, then you are under surveillance. The reasons for this sort of surveillance vary.

Surveillance for marketing purposes

Businesses collate information about you and use it to help sell their products. They can build up a personal profile from social networking sites, the products you buy and your phone records. This is called data mining. Much of this tracking is done automatically by computers. Companies hold that it is in customers' interests because it helps them to work out which products people want. However, they may actively use this information to market to customers in an intrusive way. In an extreme example, a Canadian funeral home obtained a list of people diagnosed with

case study

A life story from Facebook

People may freely choose to put information about themselves in the public domain, but they might not realize that an observer could potentially combine the details to build up a full picture of their lives. It could even present a threat to their safety. In Canada, in 2008, a newspaper reporter set out to show how easily private information can be used

for surveillance. He pieced together the life story and personal details of 17-year-old Jennifer Porter from her Facebook profile and then met up with her to show her what he had discovered. He knew her home address, mobile number, workplace, where she was going to university, what she planned to study, her hobbies and taste in books and music.

◄ Facebook has more than 500 million active users, of whom half log on to their accounts on any given day. Yet many users do not realize how much of their personal information is available to the public.

◀ Businesses still use door-to-door marketing to gain information about consumers. There are rules to protect the privacy of the people they interview.

cancer, and contacted one of them to try to sell her funeral services. Companies may also use surveillance information in underhand ways, for example, to steal product ideas from other businesses in order to undermine their competitors.

Surveillance to stop crime

Surveillance is also used to protect the public. The police may ask telephone companies to provide the call records of suspected criminals, as part of a criminal investigation. The government may investigate people's financial records to see if they are paying the correct amount of tax. Businesses may also use surveillance to look out for wrongdoing. If you make several transactions in a short space of

time, the bank may contact you to investigate in case someone has illegally obtained access to your account.

summary

▶ Definitions of privacy include privacy of information, communications and territorial privacy.

▶ Surveillance is the close observation of individuals or groups.

▶ Surveillance can be used to protect the population and also for commercial purposes, such as marketing.

CHAPTER 2

In the privacy of your own home

The Internet has changed the boundaries of privacy. Our friends, businesses, criminals and the government know far more about us than ever before. In extreme cases, when they have information that shows people might have broken the law, police officers have the right to enter people's homes and intrude directly on their private lives. Is it possible – and desirable – to maintain privacy in our homes nowadays?

Privacy and social networking

Social networking has numerous benefits. You can stay in touch with your friends and family, find out about events and organize your social life. You can choose how much information to share by using the privacy settings. Yet there are important considerations. For instance, Facebook owns all the data (text and images) users put up on their pages. Users cannot hide some of their personal information, including their profile photo and list of friends and interests. Some users may not want all of this information to be publicly available. Also, information on social networks remains there for a long time. You can delete your account, but it will remain on archived (stored) versions of websites or on other people's pages. Even if you are not on Facebook, other people can still upload photos or information about you to share on the Internet. Future employers or college admissions staff could find this information and gain

After a party, the partygoers often upload photos to social networking sites. They might not want their employer to see such photos.

▲ Employers may check the social networking sites of potential employees and discuss their activities with them at job interviews.

an impression of you based on the material they find. If this impression is negative, this could work out to the disadvantage of your application.

Privacy and business

It is extremely hard to control the amount of information that is known about you. A large quantity is collated when you are online, often without you realizing it. Search engines, such as Google, keep a record of your searches; this is called digital tracking. Many websites use cookies – small files that they install on your computer to carry information from one session to another. The next time you log in, the website already has your personal details. Businesses also collect data when you visit sites, make transactions, do online surveys and play games.

▲ Companies can gather information about their customers from their credit card purchases. If they shop with a loyalty card, the company collects data about the transactions and can build up a profile of the shopper.

Commercial companies declare that the data they gather helps them provide a better service because they understand your habits. They can offer you products or services that you might want to buy.

Some customers feel that businesses can go too far and invade people's privacy. If you buy a product or service online, often you are added to a mailing list to receive marketing messages, unless you specifically opt out. The company may share your details with others. You may receive unwanted marketing emails, calls, letters or text messages. For instance, you might buy a new kitchen and shortly afterwards, you begin to receive calls or

emails from companies trying to sell you other house renovation services.

It's a fact

Radio Frequency Identification (RFID) tags are a form of automatic identification that transmits the identity of an object or person using radio waves. Manufacturers and shops tag their products, US libraries use them to keep track of books and CDs, and people can chip their pet with an RFID tag. The further development of RFID tags could allow companies to track their product long after its purchase, which could be seen as an invasion of privacy.

▲ A young man plays poker online. Some online games require players to provide personal details, which businesses might illegally sell on to other companies.

Policing your computer

Even material on your own computer may not always be completely private. If the police suspect a person of a crime, the suspect's rights to privacy will be compromised. Police officers can covertly gain access to the individual's hard drive and read everything on the computer. This is called remote searching. The police argue this is occasionally necessary to prevent serious crime. Yet civil liberties organizations counter that it is an invasion of privacy – just like someone walking uninvited into your home, or reading your diary.

viewpoints

'We collect personal information about you for business purposes, such as evaluating your financial needs, processing your requests and transactions, informing you about products and services that may be of interest to you, and providing customer service.'
A financial company's privacy policy explains why it is necessary to collect personal information, Mark-to-Marketdebate.com, 2010

'How would you feel if you were in the mall and someone followed you around with a camera, noting every item you looked at. I'm amazed that there's this set of values out there in these companies that thinks it's okay to capture data about one's meanderings [wanderings] on the Web and attempt to make money off them without consent.'
Beth Givens, director of the Privacy Rights Clearinghouse (an organization that campaigns for consumers' privacy rights) claims that businesses infringe on the right to privacy online, msnbc.com, 2010

▲ Criminals can use a stolen passport to commit identity theft, replacing the photo with another so that a different person can adopt the victim's identity.

Criminals invading privacy

Legal companies may compromise your privacy online but, more worryingly, so too may criminals. The freedom people enjoy on the Internet has provided opportunities for dishonest people to develop tools that infringe on privacy to acquire access to their victims' money and personal information (identity fraud).

Thieves use phishing in an attempt to discover passwords that will enable them to obtain sensitive information, such as credit card details. Usually, they send an email that looks like it comes from a genuine company. The email may say there has been a problem with your account and you need to click on a link to remedy the problem. The link takes you to a spoof (fake) site, and the thief will be able to see the personal details you enter.

Identity theft

The most serious problem is identity theft – when a criminal manages to obtain key personal information from the victim, such as his or her name and address, date of birth, mother's maiden name and National Insurance number. The thief can then use that identity to open new bank accounts, buy goods and services and run up huge bills using someone else's identity. Identity theft can be done offline, too – thieves can even retrieve personal details from paperwork, such as bank statements, bills and letters that have been thrown in the bin.

It's a fact

Technology research company Gartner estimates that phishing activities cost US banks and credit card companies an estimated US$2.8 billion (£1.8 billion) a year.

case study

Falling prey to identity theft

Katie had no idea that failing to renew her PC's firewall protection could lead to identity theft. A friend of Katie's became a victim of hackers, who accessed her address book and sent out bogus emails to all her contacts. When Katie received the message, she thought it was from her friend and clicked on a link in the email. This allowed the hackers to download a code onto her PC that enabled them to retrieve her personal information.

Katie had online banking details, passwords and her National Insurance number stored on her PC. The hackers were able to steal her identity to apply for credit cards and sign up for gambling sites. She only realized what had happened when the bills started to arrive. She had to contact the credit card companies to explain and also report the crime to the police. By talking to her friend, Katie eventually worked out how her PC had been attacked and called in a computer expert to delete the harmful code and install firewall protection. Overall, the invasion of her private life was an extremely unpleasant experience that made her feel very vulnerable.

▲ Purchasing items online usually involves having to enter credit card details on the seller's site. If it is not a genuine site, hackers could steal these details.

▲ Demonstrators protest against nuclear submarines outside the Faslane Naval Base in Scotland. Anti-government protesters like these are closely monitored by the police.

Privacy and the state

We obviously do not want criminals to invade our privacy but what about the police and other state agencies? When should they be allowed to examine our personal affairs or search our homes?

Under Article 8 of the European Convention (see page 6), people have a right to respect for their home life, without interference by unlawful surveillance or entry into the house. They have the right to respect for family life, which includes any stable relationship between relatives. However, this right can be challenged by the state. For example, social services can intervene in family life to take a child into care or to deport a family member deemed to be illegally living in the country. The police have the right to intrude into homes to prevent crime. But are these intrusions always justified? For instance, a family might contest the legality of a deportation.

It's a fact

There are laws to make sure that organizations manage information about you in a fair way. The EU Data Protection Directive states that information should be collected for specified lawful reasons, should be accurate and kept securely. You have the right to find out what information is held about you and to correct any inaccurate facts. In practice, it is hard to monitor whether every organization is following these rules.

In a democracy, it is debatable whether the authorities should be allowed to search the homes of opponents of the government, such as anti-war protesters and people opposed to nuclear weapons.

case study

FBI raids anti-war activists' homes

In September 2010, the Federal Bureau of Investigation (FBI) in the US raided the homes and offices of anti-war activists in various cities across the country. They targeted especially those activists who had organized protests against the US-led war in Iraq. The police claimed that they were seeking evidence that the activists were supporting terrorist organizations in the Middle East and South America and it was necessary to search their personal affairs. In Chicago, they took away 30 boxes of papers from the homes of Stephanie Weiner and Joseph Iosbaker,

including a postcard from an old girlfriend of Iosbaker's. The police made no arrests and said the activists posed no danger to the public, but that they would sift through the papers and determine those that could provide evidence.

The activists have been involved in labour and anti-war movements for many years and denied any wrongdoing. They believed the searches were an attempt to intimidate them into stopping their campaign against US wars. Protesting government policy is not a crime in the US, so they felt the seizure of their private papers was an unjustified intrusion into their privacy.

◀ An FBI officer removes a box of documents from the home of an anti-war activist during the September 2010 raids in Watertown, Massachusetts.

summary

▶ There are advantages to sharing information on the Internet, but it is virtually impossible to control how the information is used.

▶ Criminals may invade people's privacy to steal from them.

▶ Government agencies have the right to enter private homes, but there is a debate over what is acceptable intervention.

CHAPTER 3

Schools under surveillance

The first decade of the twenty-first century has seen a rise of surveillance in schools in Europe, Australia and the US, including CCTV and biometric identification systems. Surveillance can help to provide security for staff and students. Yet it may give a false sense of security, because the technology is not foolproof and it can encroach on privacy of both teachers and pupils. In addition, young people themselves may intrude on the privacy of classmates or teachers through social networking sites.

Security systems

School students may experience various forms of surveillance for security reasons.

Some surveillance is carried out by the staff. For instance, school staff may examine student lockers and mobile phones, and search children for drugs. Metal detectors are used to find out if students are carrying knives.

Increasingly, new technologies provide security, such as CCTV cameras. The cameras are placed around the school, sometimes even in the toilets. Some education experts assert that the cameras deter students from bullying and vandalism and reduce misbehaviour in class. They cut truancy rates and deter students from smoking, because they know they will be caught on camera. CCTV can also help to

▼ At Lammas School in Leyton, UK, police use scanners to find out if the students are carrying weapons.

put off intruders from entering the school. However, others insist that CCTV cameras are extremely costly, and there is no concrete evidence that they prevent bad behaviour. Furthermore, the cameras invade privacy. The feeling of being watched all the time makes students and teachers self-conscious; they can never hold a private conversation. This constant surveillance creates an atmosphere of distrust.

CCTV cameras are regularly used in public ▶ places, as shown here, but it is only in recent years that they have been introduced into the school environment.

case study

A school security system

Arthur Phillip High School in Paramatta, Australia, promotes the use of technology in education. It has a wireless campus, and laptops are widely used in the classroom. Concerned about safety on the campus, the school introduced a new security system, integrated with their existing technology.

The new system controls all the doors and gates. When the school bell rings at break time, the gates open to let the students out. At the end of break, the bell triggers the gates to close. CCTV cameras scan the school premises, including the corridors, playgrounds and car parks, and provide high-quality images. There is a video control station in the staff room with large LCD monitors; the staff can also access the system on their iPhone or iPad while moving around the school.

Supporters of security systems say they are essential for monitoring students and settling disputes. If there is an incident in the school, teachers can look at the recorded CCTV footage and find out exactly what happened. Opponents argue it is unethical to make school like a prison, where students are tracked at every moment of the day. Unless there are severe problems in a school, such a high level of surveillance is unjustified.

ID systems

New biometric identification systems using fingerprint or iris recognition have been introduced in schools to check identity and allow access to services such as the computers or canteen. In Stockholm, Sweden, children's fingerprints are taken when they start school aged six, and pupils scan their fingertips to access the Schools Data Network. They do not need to remember a user name and password. In New Jersey, US, several schools have brought in iris-scanning equipment. Those in favour of this technology assert that it is a highly reliable method of checking identification.

However, civil liberties and some parents' groups believe that these new technologies are an unnecessary violation of privacy. According to the UK Human Rights Act (1998), any invasion of privacy must be proportionate to the threat, but the risk of children forgetting passwords or losing library cards does not seem a great threat. Also, schools have often taken children's biometric data without their parents' knowledge or consent, which is considered unethical. Furthermore, opponents question who has access to the children's private details, how securely they will be kept and for how long. They contend that school officials are not experts in using the systems and handling such sensitive data, so they cannot guarantee the safekeeping of children's records, which could be hacked into by criminals.

Strict guidelines

Could rules be established for these technologies, as has been done for older forms? For example, photographs are often taken in school for publicity purposes or to publish in local newspapers.

◀ A fingerprint scanner in operation. The scanned fingerprint will then be stored in a database and can be compared to other fingerprints already on the system.

▲ Photographs of school sports events often appear in the local newspapers. It is harder to control the digital use of images.

Clear guidelines govern the use of these photographs, and parents must give their permission for them to appear. If strict guidelines governed the use of fingerprint or iris databases, perhaps children's privacy could be respected. But the possibility remains that the systems could be open to misuse.

It's a fact

It is becoming increasingly common to use fingerprinting as a means of checking identification in schools in Western countries. The UK and US are at the forefront of using biometric technology, and fingerprinting is also used in Sweden and Belgium.

viewpoints

'After scanning staff, students, and parents, they still only had a 78% accuracy rate. Outdoor lighting, cameras freezing up or misidentifying people, and people not lining up properly were the most common problems. . . [causing] failure of the system. If the technology cannot be properly used, then it becomes a liability . . . Biometrics give parents a feeling of safety and security, but it's not guaranteed.'
A comment on the Loss of Privacy website, about the introduction of iris-scanning cameras in schools in New Egypt, New Jersey, US, 27 October 2006

'A person's iris is fully developed within 18 months after birth, and is protected by eyelashes, eyelids and the retina. Its shape hardly changes so that it has higher consistency compared to other biometric characteristics. Its higher uniqueness in shape than a face or fingerprints ensures that an authentication system using the iris [identity checking] is immensely reliable.'
The advantages of using iris recognition technology, from the website of Idteck, a company that makes security products, 2010

▲ Bullying is common in schools but cyberbullying means that victims can also be targeted at home through the Internet or their mobile phone.

Young people invading privacy

Young people themselves may intrude on the privacy of other students or school staff. They might upload pictures or videos of friends, schoolmates or teachers, for example to YouTube, or release private information about them. Internet and mobile technologies have enabled people to do this without the permission of those who feature in the images, which entails a loss of privacy.

Students may infringe on others' privacy in a deliberately nasty way by bombarding them with inappropriate texts or Facebook messages, uploading unflattering photos of them or building websites specially to bully them. This is cyberbullying. It is a serious problem because the harmful messages and images can be easily and rapidly spread to a wide audience. Also, it is hard to identify the bullies because they use false names and hide behind email addresses. To counter the problem, schools need to develop policies to control the use of technology. They can make it clear that all communications can be traced back to the source by tracking the computer's Internet Protocol (IP) address, and students who break the rules will be punished.

case study

Georgia's story

Thirteen-year-old Georgia had been popular at school but she fell out with the other girls in her group over a boy and they stopped talking to her. Her former friends began to post horrible comments on her social network page, saying she was fat and ugly. There were even threats to attack her. Georgia's behaviour changed. She became sad and withdrawn. After school, she rushed straight home to hide in her bedroom and ignored her mobile. Her mum grew worried and contacted the school, but the cyberbullying did not stop. Georgia became so desperately miserable and

felt so worthless that she even started to think about killing herself. Her mum spoke to the teachers again and this time, her daughter was given counselling, as were the bullies. School broke up for the summer, and the following term, the bullying did not reoccur.

A few months later, the charity Beatbullying visited the school. Georgia immediately volunteered to train to be a cybermentor – an online mentor who helps other children suffering from cyberbullying. Her confidence grew as she realized she could now help others to overcome these nasty invasions of privacy.

◀ Anti-bullying charities often visit schools to make them aware of what cyberbullying means and the effects it can have on the victim.

summary

▶ There has been a huge increase in surveillance in schools using new technologies; those in favour say it increases security, while opponents claim it is not always effective or secure.

▶ The use of biometric identification systems has led to an ethical debate over the invasion of privacy this may cause.

▶ Students themselves may invade privacy, in extreme cases leading to cyberbullying.

CHAPTER 4

Watched at work

Employers use surveillance to protect their premises and employees, but also to check up on their workers. Public bodies, such as local councils, may carry out surveillance of their service users as part of their job. Where should the boundary lie between the safeguarding of people and property and the unacceptable invasion of privacy?

Surveillance for protection

Businesses and public places such as hospitals and council offices use surveillance equipment, such as CCTV cameras, as well as security staff. The objective is to preserve the safety of employees and visitors, and to prevent and detect theft.

Checking up on the workers

Employers use a range of techniques to keep an eye on workers: they watch them with CCTV, listen to phone calls, observe their computer screens and monitor Internet use. They may use software that counts the key strokes of each worker to oversee performance. They may video staff to create a constant record of what they do. Workplace surveillance is intended to promote good behaviour and to provide evidence to settle any disputes.

▼ Surveillance at the workplace can include monitoring offices, corridors and even outside areas, such as car parks.

◀ This image was captured by hospital CCTV cameras and showed a suspect wanted by the police for questioning over two murders in London, in 2003.

case study

Fired after Facebook comments

A 16-year-old UK office worker lost her job after commenting on Facebook that it was boring. Kimberley had only been in the job for three weeks. She was called in to speak to the manager; another colleague was present. The manager handed her a letter and said that he had seen her comments on Facebook and did not want bad things about his company said in public. Therefore she was to lose her job.

In his view, she had showed disrespect and dissatisfaction and there was no point investing time and money training her if she was bored and likely to leave soon. Kimberley did not see it this way. She used Facebook to keep up with her friends and had made the remark to them. It was just a throwaway comment, not to be taken too seriously. Yet she had invited her new colleagues to be friends on Facebook, so they saw the post and had passed it on to their manager. This example illustrates an important effect of workplace surveillance: employees have to be extremely careful about what they say about their job – at work and outside – if this information is going to be accessible to people other than close friends.

▲ In many workplaces nowadays, workers are literally being monitored over their shoulder by cameras that video their every move.

Benefits of workplace surveillance

Surveillance allows employers to protect themselves and their property more effectively than security staff alone. It can provide evidence in legal cases. For instance, in 2004, the Australian Industrial Relations Commissions used surveillance evidence to uphold the sacking of a worker who had sent pornographic emails to a female employee. Surveillance can help employers to investigate the efficiency of their workers, and therefore their business. It allows them to track how much workers steal from the company, for example, by calling friends in work time or taking stationery. Computer-based employees may spend part of the day engaged in personal activities such as emails, online chatting or games, or downloading music. Surveillance of their screens deters such behaviour and ensures people stick to their work tasks.

viewpoints

'The main consequence of ICT surveillance has been a sharp increase in work strain (involving feelings of exhaustion, anxiety and worry related to work). . . The most adverse impact on work strain is for administrative and white-collar employees [people who do not do manual work], up 10 per cent when their performance is continually checked by ICT systems. This group includes call-centre staff, others providing telephone-based services, and those processing paperwork for entry to computer databases.'
Summary of research reported in *Market, Class, and Employment* by Patrick McGovern, Stephen Hill, Colin Mills, and Michael White, OUP, 2007

'Visible security cameras work as a deterrent to damaging and vandalizing company property. The employer has a good chance of collecting money for damages based on proof on camera of who destroyed property. If the security footage is monitored by a security guard or company, the person damaging the company's property may be caught immediately.'
Maureen Malone, eHow, 25 June 2010

The disadvantages

Despite its benefits, the use of surveillance to spy on employees is contentious. There are arguments about the effectiveness of CCTV surveillance (see page 19). The over-reliance on electronic equipment can be problematic: the equipment may be damaged or go wrong. Workers may see surveillance as a violation of privacy, causing stress, lowering morale and making them resent their employer. Employers may abuse the laws governing surveillance, for example, by using covert surveillance in private areas such as shower rooms and toilets. Surveillance can affect the relationship of trust between employer and employees, creating tension and suspicion. These negative aspects can create a bad atmosphere in the workplace, which may make workers less productive. Companies may even use surveillance information to fire unwanted workers. For example, a 2004 report by the Council for Civil Liberties in New South Wales, Australia, related that private investigators had been asked to place individual workers under surveillance to find evidence against them.

It's a fact

Laws restrict the use of staff monitoring by employers. In the US, for example, employers can openly or covertly place cameras in public spaces, but it is illegal to covertly video workers in places where they can expect privacy, such as in the toilets. Employers can monitor emails and telephone calls that are for the purpose of the business, but may only examine the equipment that they own.

▼ These call-centre workers are closely monitored. Their employers are entitled to listen to their calls to check they are following the proper procedures.

Snooping on the public

As well as surveilling staff, public bodies may snoop on the public as part of their job. In the UK, local councils utilize covert surveillance to check up on people who might be breaking the rules. They track parents who are accused of cheating the school entrance system by pretending to live in a different area, and those who illegally dump rubbish or allow their dogs to foul the streets. The councils maintain that this is necessary to catch offenders, while critics assert that the intervention is too heavy-handed for such relatively minor offences.

◄ In areas where people dump large amounts of rubbish, local councils argue they are justified in using surveillance to try to catch the culprits.

Sharing information

Public bodies, such as councils, increasingly share the information they collect about people. In Australia, information supplied to a public-sector organization for one purpose is often transferred to other agencies; for instance, health, education and transport departments share data. This is partly because some benefits relate to more than one organization. If you're a student, you are entitled to reduced fares on public transport. Also, the records of people who receive government benefits are handed to the police to probe for fraud. In the UK, a national health database with all citizens' health records is under development; the police will eventually have access to it.

Privacy campaigners declare that this sharing of information is an unethical invasion of privacy because people have not given permission for their details to be transferred. However, the combining of records can make services more efficient and help the government to prevent cheating. This is necessary to run fair and effective public services and save money.

Information may be shared with the general public too. In the US for example, registers of convicted sex offenders are freely available online. Some websites mesh geographical data with the registers to produce maps of where the offenders live. The information is provided to protect the public, making them aware of any offender living nearby. However, the accuracy of the data cannot be guaranteed. It could allow people to inflict additional punishment on an offender – or a person they believe is an offender.

It's a fact

In the US, the Fourth Amendment of the Constitution protects citizens against unreasonable searches of a person's property, including documents. However, the Supreme Court has held that any information that people give to banks, schools, businesses or even doctors is not covered, because they volunteered to supply that information to a third party. Furthermore, government data mining computer programmes can trawl though personal, financial, travel and medical records to try to identify patterns of behaviour that might reveal criminal activity.

summary

▶ Workplace surveillance helps employers to protect their staff and property, as well as to observe their workers.

▶ Surveillance can increase workers' stress levels and lead to mistrust between employers and employees.

▶ Local councils may use covert surveillance and record sharing to check up on service users. This can make services more efficient, but may violate people's privacy.

CHAPTER 5

Privacy and the media

By law, journalists are supposed to weigh up the right of the public to know about events against the right of the individuals involved to privacy and fair treatment. Yet this does not always happen in practice.

Your right to privacy

According to Article 8 of the European Convention of Human Rights (see page 6), the publication of stories about your private life can breach your right to privacy. For example, confidential information, such as personal diaries or health records, should generally not be released to the public.

Journalists and reporters working for high-quality media companies consider carefully whether exposing a story is in the public interest or an intrusion into private life. However, many others are less concerned with fairness and just want to sell a good story. Sensationalist stories help to sell newspapers and increase the ratings for TV programmes.

It's a fact

In the US, the First Amendment to the Constitution allows for the freedom of speech and of the press, which shields the media from government interference. The press does not have complete freedom though. There are laws to prevent the invasion of privacy and libel (printing untrue statements about people), and restrictions on what reporters are allowed to do to obtain a story.

◀ Newspapers and magazines at a news stand in Mexico. Newspapers often have sensational stories on the front cover to encourage people to buy them.

One example is the story of a girl aged just ten, who had a baby with her 13-year-old boyfriend in Spain. A UK newspaper, the *Daily Mail*, published photos of the young couple, while a Spanish newspaper printed photos of the newborn child. For the newspapers, this was an extraordinary event that would fascinate their readers. However, the authorities in Seville, southern Spain, where the girl lived, decided to take legal action against the newspapers for invading the privacy of a minor. Was it right for the papers to print the story on the grounds of public interest, or was it unjust to intrude on the privacy of the girl, who could suffer from widespread publicity about her difficult situation?

case study

The murderers of Jamie Bulger

In the UK in 1993, two ten-year-old boys, Jon Venables and Robert Thompson, kidnapped two-year-old Jamie Bulger. They subjected him to cruel torture, throwing bricks at him and beating him with a metal bar. After bludgeoning him to death, they hid Jamie's body on a railway line. The violent young killers were caught and sent to prison until they were 18. Then they were released with new identities and given a second chance. The publication of details that could reveal their whereabouts was prohibited, defending their privacy. However, in 2010, when he was 27 years old, Jon Venables committed an offence that breached the terms of his release and was sent back to prison. A public debate ensued over whether the details of the offence should be made known or whether the murderer's privacy should be maintained.

▲ This grainy CCTV footage shows Jamie Bulger being led away by one of his kidnappers.

▲ Public figures and celebrities are continually photographed by paparazzi – photojournalists who specialize in selling photos of the rich and famous to newspapers. Paparazzi are often accused of invading people's privacy.

Public figures and privacy

There is a particular debate about the privacy of politicians, celebrities and sports personalities. Some people insist they have the same right to privacy as others because what they do in their private lives does not directly affect how they do their job. However, others claim that the public has a right to know about their private lives; they use the media to advance their careers, so they should accept public examination. Royal families are another example: ordinary citizens pay taxes that help to maintain them, so it could be argued that they have a right to know the details of royal lives. The media go to great lengths to unearth stories about royals, believing this is in the public interest. For example, in 2007, the royal editor of the UK newspaper the *News of the World* was jailed for hacking into the voicemail messages of royal aides, an illegal breach of personal privacy.

Another debate centres on types of privacy, such as financial privacy. We know how much government workers earn, such as politicians, because we pay for their salaries from taxes. Is this fair or does it violate their financial privacy? Should the salaries of those working for private companies be kept private?

It may be in the public interest to know. In the US, for instance, nine banks with financial difficulties received US$175 billion of US government aid in 2008. That year, those banks paid out US$32.6 billion in bonuses to their employees – rewarding them with money from people's taxes.

Complicated issues like these make it hard to make rules about privacy and the media. There is a debate over where the balance lies between individuals' rights and journalists' rights to freedom of expression, as well as the public's right to knowledge and information.

▲ Andy Coulson leaves 10 Downing Street, the prime minister's home, after resigning from his job for the second time over phone-hacking allegations in January 2011.

case study

News of the World phone-hacking scandal

In 2007, the royal editor of the UK newspaper *News of the World* was jailed for hacking into the voicemail messages of royal aides. It is illegal for people other than the government or police to gain access to another person's telephone and a clear breach of personal privacy. Andy Coulson, the paper's editor, said it was a one-off case but he took responsibility and resigned.

Two years later, the *Guardian* newspaper claimed that reporters from *News of the World* had hacked the phones of up to 3,000 media celebrities, sports stars and politicians. The police looked into the matter but decided no investigation was needed. However, in 2010, new allegations about widespread phone hacking emerged, and the police reopened their inquiries. In January 2011, Andy Coulson, now the government's director of communications, was forced to resign once more.

summary

▶ Journalists have to weigh up individuals' right to privacy with the public's right to know.

▶ There is debate over the degree of privacy that public figures should enjoy.

▶ It is a breach of privacy laws to access someone's voicemail messages without their consent. This is called phone hacking and can lead to imprisonment.

CHAPTER 6

On the streets: surveillance to prevent crime

In the attempt to prevent crime, the police use surveillance on the streets to scan for suspicious activity. They install CCTV cameras, profile certain communities and track people on the move. Is the level of surveillance justified or is it an unnecessary breach of privacy?

Surveillance of public places

The police use surveillance on the streets and in shopping centres. CCTV cameras have increasingly been adopted in Western countries to deter and detect crime. The evidence from CCTV footage is useful for identifying criminals, but whether the cameras actually prevent crime is unproven. Surveys show that people feel safer if there are CCTV cameras, but concerns have been raised about intrusion into privacy, especially now that the video images are quite clear, thanks to improvements in surveillance technology. Cases of misuse of the images have been recorded. For instance, male operators have been caught zooming in on images of young women for their own pleasure. Some CCTV cameras can record conversations between members of the public and new software will allow them to detect anyone behaving suspiciously on the street. This could lead to a huge

◀ CCTV cameras are a common sight in Western cities. The UK has the highest density of CCTV cameras in the world.

▲ When police officers stop a suspect on the street, they can input the individual's details on a handheld device and connect to the police database to find out if the person has been involved in a crime.

invasion of people's privacy when out and about. Because although CCTV footage can offer important information if a criminal act is caught on camera, the majority of filming will be of people going about their lives, possibly not even aware of being observed.

Video surveillance

As well as using CCTV, police officers video the public at events such as sports matches and demonstrations and keep the footage on databases. The police contend that this provides a record of the event that can be used if the law is broken. However, the police have in some cases presented video evidence in court showing protesters attacking police during a confrontation, but omitting police assaults on demonstrators. Civil rights campaigners claim that it is unethical both to video everyone attending such events and to edit the footage so that it is misleading.

viewpoints

'CCTV cameras represent a substantial threat to individual privacy and to the exercise of rights such as freedom of expression and freedom of association. As a consequence, it is vital that those responsible for the management and operation of these systems are aware of the dangers of public area surveillance, and that they work to ensure that CCTV does not threaten fundamental human rights.'
Benjamin J. Goold, University of British Columbia, Canada, 2010

'The ability for CCTV footage to convince offenders to plead guilty did appear to save police and court time. Half of the respondents (49 per cent) said that CCTV had helped them to secure a guilty plea within the last month. . . "If the evidence is good, nine out of ten admit to the offence."
(patrol sergeant)'
Police attitudes to and use of CCTV by Tom Levesley and Amanda Martin, Home Office UK, 2005

Police profiling

The police also try to prevent crime and terrorism by surveilling groups of people they believe are likely to break the law. This is called profiling. The police claim that this is intelligent policing. For example, they carry out surveillance of people in areas with a high level of drug abuse. They keep an eye on suspected drug dealers, which can lead to arrests.

Profiling travellers and Muslim communities

Since the 9/11 terrorist attacks, the police in Western countries have increased the profiling of travellers flying abroad, because terrorists are likely to travel for training to plan their strikes, as well as be on that mode of transport for their actual attack. For example, the US has introduced the US-VISIT system. Immigration officers collect biometrics – digital fingerprints and a photograph – from all international visitors to the country. This enables them to accurately identify people and decide whether they pose a risk to the US. Within Western countries, the police observe Muslim areas, organizations and individuals because terrorist attacks have been committed by Muslim extremists in the past. Activities in mosques are monitored to find out if people are spreading anti-Western views.

However, many civil rights campaigners believe that profiling stereotypes particular communities as likely to commit crime, although the vast majority are law-abiding. Likewise, it treats all travellers as potential criminals. Campaigners believe it is an unnecessary infringement of privacy.

▼ A US immigration officer operates the US-VISIT system, collecting biometric data from a visitor.

case study

Profiling Muslim communities

After two unexploded bombs were discovered in London in 2007, the police in Birmingham, central England, installed covert CCTV cameras in the Muslim areas of Birmingham, to enable them to carry out surveillance operations against suspected terrorists.

The scheme aroused great anger among Muslims, who had not been consulted and felt that as a community they were being targeted as potential terrorists. The police assured them that the cameras were never switched on, and in 2010, agreed to withdraw them. However, a number of terrorist suspects have been arrested in these Muslim areas. Some people contended that the civil liberties of the victims of future terrorist attacks were more important than the civil liberties of those who disliked and opposed the CCTV surveillance.

▲ Some of the CCTV cameras installed in the predominantly Muslim communities of Washwood Heath and Sparbrook were placed in covert spots, such as high up in trees.

summary

▶ The police use CCTV cameras to carry out surveillance in public places, but their usefulness in deterring crime is debated.

▶ Although people may feel safer where there are CCTV cameras, there are concerns that they may invade privacy.

▶ The police profile travellers and certain communities to prevent crime, but civil rights campaigns argue this stereotypes these groups and may not be effective anyway.

CHAPTER 7

Crime prevention behind the scenes

The 9/11 attacks have led Western countries to expand behind-the-scenes surveillance. Internet surveillance is commonly used in crime prevention, while other methods, including wiretapping (listening in to people's phone conversations), are deployed to track individual suspects. The police have built up DNA databases to store information about suspects. Is this surveillance in the public interest or are people's civil liberties being breached?

Internet surveillance

The US is at the forefront of promoting electronic surveillance technologies. Its government has insisted that all new technologies have to allow surveillance.

▼ Police officers remove evidence during a search of an Internet café in Valencia, Spain, in 2009. The search followed the arrest of several people accused of forging documents for the terrorist organization al Qaeda.

For instance, wireless technology is used to retrieve material on computers and mobile phones, while 'black boxes' can monitor traffic in and out of particular computer networks. The government can compel search engines such as Google to track the activities of suspects, and the police can intercept and read emails. Other Western countries have adopted similar measures.

There are many good reasons for surveillance on the Internet. The majority of people agree that it is right for the police to scan for websites that promote racial hatred or terrorism and for networks of paedophiles who exchange child pornography. Yet many would disagree with the tracking of people who hold different views from the government. Huge numbers of organizations are surveilled, including legal anti-government protest movements and those belonging to minority communities. This intrusion into people's online activities may lead to wrong accusations. Is it acceptable in democratic countries to monitor such groups?

case study

Politics student arrested

In 2008, a student at the University of Nottingham in England was arrested, along with a member of staff, on suspicion of possessing terrorist materials. Rizwaan Sabir, a politics student, had downloaded an edited version of the al Qaeda handbook from a US government website.

A junior member of staff had spotted the suspicious material on the computer and called the police. The police arrested Sabir and a staff member and searched campus property, believing the pair could be part of an al-Qaeda terrorist cell. They detained the men for six days before releasing them without charge. It turned out that Mr Sabir was studying terrorism for his dissertation (long essay) and had sent the al Qaeda document to the staff member to print out. Many students and staff at Nottingham were shocked that the finding of the document on a computer triggered immediate police involvement. A simple conversation with the student's supervisor would have resolved the question of why he was using extremist material.

▲ Rizwaan Sabir used al Qaeda documents as part of his research into Islam in government policy, which focused on counter-terrorism.

Individuals under the spotlight

Police forces can apply for special legal powers in order to place suspected criminals under constant surveillance. Governments also spy on potential enemies of the state. A common way to track individuals is through wiretapping. As well as acquiring access to landline calls, the police may ask mobile-phone companies for lists of the calls suspects have made and information to track their movements. Since each mobile gives out a signal, it is easy to locate the user. The police can build up a detailed profile from an individual's mobile use.

The police may use audio bugging, too – placing a tiny electronic bug in a person's home, for example hidden in an object, such as a sports trophy. The bug has its own power supply and can remain active for ten years.

Governments recognize that such surveillance powers should be used only in exceptional circumstances to counter threats to society – and that illegal surveillance should be heavily punished. But privacy campaigners believe that larger numbers of people are surveilled than necessary, which severely restricts their freedom.

An extraordinary case of modern-day spying came to light in 2010. In the US, the Federal Bureau of Investigation (FBI) uncovered a Russian spy ring. A team of

▲ This bugging equipment was used by the security forces in former Communist East Germany. Privacy campaigners in Germany today are concerned that the increase in surveillance is turning their country into a watched society like East Germany.

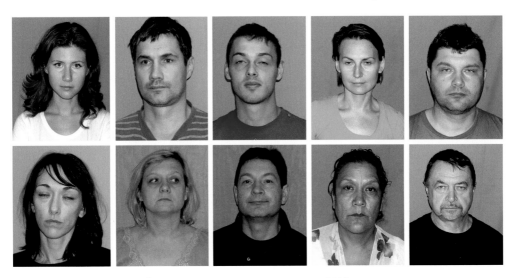

▲ The police photographs of the ten Russians arrested in the US in 2010.
They were returned to their country in exchange for Russia's release of
four prisoners on charges of spying for the West.

ten agents had been living under cover
for nearly 20 years in the US. The FBI
alleged that the spies had succeeded in
befriending a scientist working on nuclear
bombs and a financier (expert in
managing money) with important political
ties. Yet it appeared they had not
unearthed information of great value to
Russia. More typical of professional spying
today is the tracking of potential terrorists.

It's a fact

In the US, wiretapping and the interception
of phones and computer communications is
legal if such interception could provide
evidence of a broad range of crimes,
including terrorism, murder, spying,
kidnapping, fraud and the violation of
trade secrets.

viewpoints

'The threat to our country has made it
necessary to give the BKA [the Federal
Crime Office] such rights to counter
threats. It is an important building
block for Germany's security architecture.'
Wolfgang Schäuble, the German interior minister,
justifies giving the BKA more legal powers to carry out
video, online and phone surveillance to investigate
suspected terrorists and criminals,
New York Times, 4 June 2008

'No matter what we do, to whom we
talk to, or who we call, in what groups
we are engaged in and what interests we
follow – the "big brother" state and the
"little brothers and sisters" in the business
sector are always one step ahead and know
better. The subsequent lack of privacy and
confidentiality endangers our society.
People who permanently feel that they
are being watched and monitored are
restrained from standing up for their
rights and a just society in an unbiased
and courageous manner.'
Call from the German website *Freiheitsredner* (Voice of
Freedom) to Europeans to demonstrate for 'Freedom
Not Fear' on 11 September, 2010

▲ In the UK, when a person is arrested for a crime, even a minor crime such as spray-painting graffiti, his or her details are entered into the DNA crime database.

Uses of DNA databases

Another vital element in surveillance is the storing of biometric data. In many countries, police officers test suspects' DNA and keep it on DNA databases. They contend that DNA tests are reliable if they are properly carried out and can help the police to solve crimes.

There are observers who argue that everyone in the population should be on the DNA database, because sometimes people commit crime even if they have never done so in the past. This would be fairer than having a database only of people who have been arrested, many of whom are later proven innocent.

viewpoints

'The DNA of innocent people should not be kept by police. People feel it is an invasion of their privacy, and there is no evidence that removing from the DNA database people who have not been charged or convicted will lead to serious crimes going undetected.'
Hugh Whittall, Director of the Nuffield Council on Bioethics, UK, contends that if charges against a suspect are dropped, the person's DNA should be removed from the database, BBC News, 4 Dec 2008

'(a) DNA is an invaluable technology in solving serious crime; but (b) as soon as you confine it to certain classes of people you produce arbitrariness [unfairness] and injustice. If everyone is on, everyone is equally treated: it would cease to be a stigma [disgrace] and instead becomes an honourable means by which everyone makes a contribution towards protecting the vulnerable from violent crime.'
Gavin Phillipson argues for a complete DNA database, *Guardian*, 19 Nov 2009

Dangers of databases

However, some privacy campaigners believe that DNA databases should contain only the DNA of convicted criminals (people found guilty of crime) rather than all suspects, including people who have been proven innocent. They are especially concerned about the keeping of DNA samples from innocent young people. In the UK, for instance, a 13-year-old girl was arrested in 2005 for throwing a snowball at a police car, and her DNA was recorded. Privacy campaigners argued against this.

In addition, there are worries that DNA tests could be unreliable; the samples may not be correctly stored or the people analysing them could make mistakes. Also, the police cannot always rely on DNA evidence, because hardened criminals find ways to avoid leaving DNA samples at the scene of the crime, for instance by wearing gloves and masks.

▲ Here a police officer fingerprints a motorist using a mobile scanner.

It's a fact

Each person's DNA is unique, except for that of identical twins. This means that DNA evidence collected from a crime scene can implicate or eliminate a suspect. Evidence from one crime scene can be compared to the evidence from another to link crimes to the same suspect.

summary

▶ The police use Internet surveillance to prevent crime but they also monitor legal anti-government and minority organizations.

▶ The police can track individuals they believe present a danger to society yet privacy campaigners believe that they surveille more people than necessary.

▶ DNA databases help the police to solve crime although there is a debate about which groups should be included in the database.

CHAPTER 8

Privacy and surveillance in the future

New commercial and surveillance technologies can bring benefits, but could come at a cost to privacy. The following are just a few examples of current developments.

Interactive TV and 'T-commerce' will allow viewers to interact with each other, make purchases via the TV and rent films on demand – this could be extremely convenient. Yet it turns George Orwell's vision of a TV that can watch you into a reality (see viewpoints panel opposite).

Face-recognition technology is developing fast. It allows the covert identification of people in public. Potentially useful for crime prevention, it also means that people could be tracked as they go about their normal business on the streets. This could be seen as an invasion of privacy.

RFID technology is likely to become cheaper and more widespread. If companies tracked their products after they were bought, they could garner valuable marketing information about the use of the goods. In this way, companies could also follow the movements of their consumers, who might not be aware of this intrusion of privacy.

▼ Interactive TV will become increasingly important and it is likely that the functions of computers and TVs will merge. While offering many opportunities, such developments will affect people's privacy.

State control or controls on the state?

Governments intend to make full use of the potential to combine databases of people's private records for the provision of services. The EU is keen on the idea of 'e-government' cards. Each person would have one card, allowing the use of state services including education, healthcare and libraries. Perhaps all state-run systems could be on one card, including ID, passport, driving licence, health record and e-government, giving officials access to all of this data. This might seem sensible, but the information could potentially be misused, for example, if an undemocratic government came to power that did not tolerate certain groups of people. Should there be more regulation of surveillance powers to control the information that is held about us and preserve some personal privacy? Could we end up living in a society that carries out perpetual surveillance of its citizens, like in George Orwell's novel *1984*? This is a crucial and urgent issue for society.

v i e w p o i n t s

'There was of course no way of knowing whether you were being watched at any given moment. . . It was even conceivable that they watched everybody all the time. But at any rate they could plug into your wire whenever they wanted to. You had to live – did live, from habit that became instinct – in the assumption that every sound you made was overheard, and except in darkness, every movement scrutinized [examined].'

George Orwell's book *1984*, published in 1949, describes a fictional society in which people are under constant surveillance and have no freedom.

'Talk of Britain sliding into a police state is daft scaremongering, but even were it true there is a mechanism to prevent it – democratic elections. People have the power to vote out administrations which they believe are heavyhanded.'

Former UK Justice Secretary Jack Straw, *Guardian*, 27 February 2009

▼ In this still from the 1984 film of *1984*, Winston Smith (John Hurt) writes a secret diary out of view of the TV that is able to observe him.

Glossary

Abuse Harmful use of something or harming other people.

Al Qaeda A radical Islamic movement, prepared to use violence to achieve its aims. It has many groups worldwide.

Biometric identification Checking identity by using a stored scan of a person's physical feature, such as a fingerprint or the iris.

Bugging Using a device to listen secretly to a person's conversations.

CCTV Closed-Circuit Television. A system using video cameras to monitor a specific area and transmit the images to a control centre.

Civil liberties The rights of people to say or do what they want while respecting others and staying within the law.

Constitution A set of laws governing a country or organization.

Counter-terrorism Action taken to prevent the activities of political groups that use violence to try to achieve their aims.

Covert Secret.

Custody The legal right to care for someone.

Cyberbullying Using electronic technology, such as email, instant messaging, websites or texts, to bully someone.

Database A set of data stored on a computer that can be looked at and used in different ways.

Data mining Looking at large amounts of information that has been collected on a computer and using it to discover patterns that can be used for marketing, crime detection or other purposes.

Domestic violence Threatening behaviour or violence against another member of a household.

DNA The chemical in the cells of animals and plants that carries genetic information. Except for identical twins, each person's DNA is unique.

DNA database A database containing DNA profiles of people arrested by the police.

EU Directive A set of privacy requirements, adopted in 1998, that ordered European nations to put the requirements into their own national law.

Fingerprint recognition Using a stored scan of a person's fingerprint to check identity.

Firewall Part of a computer system that stops other people from gaining information on your computer without permission.

Fraud The crime of deceiving someone in order to obtain money or goods illegally.

Hacker A person who gains access to information on another person's computer without permission.

Identity theft Using someone else's personal information, such as name, credit card number and passport details, without that person's knowledge, to illegally obtain money, goods or services.

Iris recognition Using a stored scan of the iris, the round, coloured part of a person's eye, to check identity.

Marketing Presenting, advertising and selling a company's products.

Paedophile A person who is sexually attracted to children.

Phishing Sending emails pretending to be a trustworthy company in order to acquire sensitive information such as user names, passwords and credit card details.

Privacy Not being watched or disturbed by other people.

Radio Frequency Identification (RFID) tag An automatic identification system that transmits the identity of an object or person using radio waves.

Suicide-bomb attack A terrorist attack in which the attacker kills themself, as well as the intended victims.

Surveillance Close observation, especially of a suspected person or group, and of places where crime may be committed. Businesses also undertake surveillance.

Terrorist A person who uses violent actions to achieve political aims.

Tracking Following the movements of somebody or something, especially by using special electronic equipment.

Wiretapping The use of an electronic or mechanical device for secretly listening to other people's telephone conversations.

Timeline

1583–90 Sir Francis Walsingham devotes himself to spying to detect conspiracies against Queen Elizabeth I of England.

1881–1917 In Russia, the Okhrana secret police organization carries out surveillance of left-wing groups to try to combat revolutionary activities.

1900 The Danish engineer Valdemar Poulson demonstrates the principle of magnetic recording, which leads to the development of magnetic tape for recording sound.

1949 George Orwell's book *1984* is published. The novel describes a society in which people are under constant surveillance.

1969 The first RFID tags are created.

1970s The Internet emerges in the US.

1980s CCTV cameras are introduced in a small number of UK towns and cities.

1984 Professor Sir Alec Jeffreys from Leicester University, UK pioneers DNA fingerprinting.

Early 1990s The general public gain access to the Internet.

1990s RFID tags are increasingly used.

1995 The first iris-recognition system becomes available for purchase.

1998 The European Convention of Human Rights states that people have the 'right to respect for private and family life, home and correspondence.'

1999 Eagan High School in Minnesota, US is one of the first schools to use fingerprint scans for checking out books from the library.

2001 Face-recognition technology is used to identify fans at the Super Bowl in Tampa, Florida, US.

(11 Sep) 19 terrorists kill nearly 3,000 people in coordinated suicide-bomb attacks on the US.

(26 Oct) The US government passes the US Patriot Act to expand the electronic surveillance of US citizens and foreign residents.

2004 The US introduces the US-VISIT system: biometric data is collected from all international visitors.

(4 Feb) Harvard University student Mark Zuckerberg launches Facebook.

(11 Mar) A series of terrorist attacks on trains in Madrid, Spain kill 191 and injure 1,841 people.

2005 (7 July) Suicide-bomb attacks in London kill 52 people and injure more than 770.

(21 July) A planned terrorist attack on the London transport system fails.

(22 July) London police kill Brazilian electrician Jean Charles de Menezes; inaccurate surveillance data led them to mistake his identity for that of a terrorist.

2007 (26 Jan) Clive Goodman, the royal editor of the UK News of the World, is sentenced to four months in prison for illegally intercepting phone messages.

(Aug) The US introduces electronic passports, with a computer chip storing the owner's data and photograph. The photo allows biometric comparison using facial recognition technology.

2008 (June) The German government adopts the BKA law, allowing the Federal Crime Office a wide range of powers to monitor and spy on the German population.

2010 All US states have their own Automated Fingerprint Identification System databases.

(11 Sept) Around 10,000 people attend the 'Freedom not Fear' protest in Berlin, Germany to protest the spread of surveillance by governments and businesses.

Further information

Books to read:

Do We Have a Right to Privacy? by Kate Shuster (Heinemann Library, 2008)

Privacy and Surveillance by Lisa Firth (Independence Educational Publishers, 2009)

Security V Privacy by Rebecca Stefoff (Benchmark Books, 2007)

Useful organizations:

The Information Commissioner's Office (ICO)

www.ico.gov.uk

Promotes openness by public bodies and data privacy.

International Debate Education Association (IDEA)

www.idebate.org

Topics for debate, including 'warrantless wiretapping', 'privacy vs security' and 'Should celebrities have greater protection from the media?'

Privacy International

www.privacyinternational.org

A human rights group that acts as a watchdog on surveillance and the invasion of privacy.

Index

Ethical Debates

Contents of new titles in the series: